Nonprofit Quick Guide™

Raising Lots of Money: Essential Measures to Grow Your Finances and Excel at Fundraising

Joanne Oppelt, MHA
Linda Lysakowski, ACFRE

Nonprofit Quick Guide: Raising Lots of Money: Essential Measures to Grow Your Finances and Excel at Fundraising

One of the **Nonprofit Quick Guide**™ series

Published by Joanne Oppelt Consulting, LLC

ISBN Print Book: 978-1-951978-21-1

13 12 11 10 9 8 7 6 5 4 3 2 1

About the Authors

JOANNE OPPELT, MHA

Joanne, principal of Joanne Oppelt Consulting, LLC, is the creator of The Sustainable High ROI Fundraising System. She is a seasoned rainmaker with a distinguished track record of success. During her twenty-five-plus years working in the nonprofit arena, she built successful fundraising programs at every stop, helping numerous agencies grow and advance their missions.

Joanne has worked with local, regional, national, and international nonprofits, helping them increase their net income and realize higher returns on their investments, resulting in continuous net surpluses. She has held positions from volunteer to executive director to consultant, working in both small and large organizations in a variety of fields including the arts, child welfare, disabilities, early childhood education, maternal and child health, mental health, public health, and at-risk youth. Her extensive background with various agencies in a variety of work roles enables her to understand the challenges nonprofits face–both internally and externally.

Joanne is the author of four books and coauthor of fourteen. She has taught at Kean University as an Adjunct Professor in its graduate program. She is also a highly sought-after speaker and presenter.

Joanne holds a master's degree in health administration from Wilkes University, where she graduated with distinction. Her bachelor's degree is in education, with a minor in psychology.

LINDA LYSAKOWSKI, ACFRE

Linda is one of approximately one hundred professionals worldwide to hold the Advanced Certified Fundraising Executive designation. Linda is the author of ten nonfiction books, a contributing author, co-editor, or coauthor of twenty-five others. She has also written seven books in the spiritual and fiction realms.

Linda has more than thirty years in the development field. She worked for a university and a museum before starting her own consulting firm. In her twenty-eight years as a philanthropic consultant, Linda has managed capital campaigns that have raised more than $50 million, helped hundreds of nonprofit organizations achieve their development goals, and trained more than forty thousand development professionals in most of the fifty states of the United States, Canada, Mexico, Egypt, and Bermuda.

She served on the Association of Fundraising Philanthropy (AFP) Foundation for Philanthropy Board and on the Professional Advancement Division for AFP. She is a past president of the Eastern Pennsylvania and Sierra (Nevada) AFP chapters. She received the Outstanding Fundraiser of the Year award from the Eastern Pennsylvania, Las Vegas, and Sierra (Nevada) chapters of AFP, was honored with the Barbara Marion Award for Outstanding Service to AFP, and received the Lifetime Achievement Award from the Las Vegas AFP chapter.

Linda is a *magna cum laude* graduate of Alvernia University with majors in banking/finance, and theology/philosophy, and a minor in communications. As a graduate of AFP's Faculty Training Academy, she is a Master Teacher.

Dedication

This book is dedicated to the nonprofit finance, marketing, and fundraising professionals who patiently and painstakingly develop, record, and review the details that are behind their organizations' success.

Contents

Chapter One

Why Gauges Are Indispensable

Data may not be the most exciting part of fundraising but gathering and analyzing it is crucial to fundraising success. Data is used in budgeting, evaluating, goal setting, benchmarking, and problem-solving. It is data that tells us what is going well and what isn't–and why, if we ask the right questions. The knowledge we use to steward our resources efficiently and raise the most money allows us to meet more mission. Always remember that it is mission and not money that you are after. Money is a vehicle to meet mission. Your donors want to make an impact in the community, not balance a checkbook. So, always put mission first. Always.

So, when are you supposed to collect and analyze data with the limited time you have? You are, after all, a busy professional who would probably much rather pursue your next request for funding than gather and interpret numbers. Your nonprofit, after all, needs the money more than the analysis of facts and figures. Right?

No, not right. To be the most effective fundraiser you can, you need a way to establish attainable goals and set reasonable expectations, then communicate them to your team. You also need to measure your agency's performance against them. The old adage, "what gets measured, gets done," is true.

If you're methodical about it and incorporate data collection into your fundraising efforts, you will have an easy way to gather as much data as you want. It's essential to measure leading indicators, those that help predict results, and not just trailing indicators, those that measure performance retrospectively. In other words, set up systems that allow you to measure success "upstream" instead of waiting until the end of the year to say, "Whoops, we didn't meet our goals."

The trick is not in collecting the data. The trick is knowing what kind of data to collect. You want to collect the data to tell you what you need to know using the least amount of resources while maintaining its validity and reliability. In other words, you want to collect data in the easiest way possible with the most understandable results while still maintaining the accuracy of your findings.

To set up that kind of system, we need to understand what is critical to know. Some of what we measure is obvious, some not.

Measuring Financial Results

The most obvious metrics are your financial metrics. You were, after all, hired to raise money. You are keenly aware of how important your fundraising efforts are to your nonprofit's ability to meet its budget. So, the most obvious data that you need is financial.

Please, please have a development budget, including both anticipated income and expected expenses. A development budget is not telling your development office to just "raise as much as you can and spend as little as you can." You will need a copy of your development budget to measure your actual revenues compared to the budget. You will also want to know how your expenses compared to the budget. If you are an executive director with a small agency, your development budget may be part of your overall budget.

You will also want to know when revenues and expenses are coming in and going out. In addition to a revenue and expense budget, you will want a cash flow projection. Cash is king. You need money to pay your bills. Make sure to coordinate your schedule of fundraising activities with your finance director so that your agency doesn't end up folding because of a cash flow deficiency. Throughout the book, we will be talking about how what you do pertains to the bottom line. However, we specifically focus on revenue metrics in **Chapter Two** and incurring expenses in **Chapter Four**.

Measuring Performance

In addition to the budget, you will want to compare your financial performance against the industry norm and against past performance. For nonfinancial indicators, you will want to compare your performance against your goals, industry norms, and past performance. You are looking for trends that can help you project future performance, formulate attainable goals, and set reasonable organizational expectations. We give average industry performance metrics throughout this book.

Measuring Efficient Use of Resources

Some fundraising activities are more efficient in their use of resources than others. For example, certain fundraising channels yield a higher profit margin and return on investment than others. An often-overlooked way to raise more money is to calculate the profit margin and return on investment for each fundraising method and change your development plan to yield the highest return on investment. This way, you are intentionally changing your mix of activities, not on someone's whim, but on data that supports the decisions you make. We talk about profit margin and return on investment in **Chapter Seven**.

Measuring Effectiveness of Methods

How much money you bring in and how efficiently you use resources are not the only essential metrics. You also need to know how effective the methods you are using to achieve your results are. And it's not pure fundraising methodology that determines the success of your outcome. If you want to raise the most community support, financial and otherwise, you need a coordinated approach. For example, you need to send effective messages that communicate your nonprofit's brand and employ smart marketing techniques that help you reach your target audiences. You may be satisfied with the results you have now. However, if your agency is to grow, it will need the community support and finances to do it. We talk about the most useful fundraising metrics in **Chapter Three** and fundraising-enhancing marketing metrics in **Chapters Five** and **Six**.

Throughout the book, we will be giving industry metrics that are accurate as of printing. Over the years, these metrics have changed a few percentage points up or down over the years, but they have remained relatively stable.

Also, we will be providing ideas on how to easily collect the data you need to analyze and predict your agency's fundraising performance. The key to keeping up with the data is regular and accurate data entry and recordkeeping. Not our favorite part of fundraising either, but very necessary to our success.

Wrapping It Up

- Knowing the questions you want answered is the first step to collecting relevant data.
- Incorporate data collection into the design of your fundraising activities.
- To set reasonable expectations with credibility, base your fundraising projections on objective data.
- Measure your results against your budget, goals, industry averages, and agency history.

◆ Plan your fundraising activities to coordinate with and leverage organizational finance, marketing, and communication efforts.

◆ Keep up with your data entry and recordkeeping.

Chapter Two

How Are You Doing Overall?

When a company is trying to realize more revenues from sales, two factors affect the outcome: price and volume. To make more money, either more people will buy the product, or people will pay more for the product, or some combination of the two. The same principle applies in fundraising: more people will give to your nonprofit or give at higher amounts, or some combination of the two. There are only two variables: the amount of donations and the number of donors. We must look at the amount of dollars raised *and* the number of donors giving to maximally influence our results. The goal, of course, is to have the highest amount of donations from the greatest number of donors.

Measuring Dollars Raised

Total dollars raised is probably the most common way people measure fundraising success. How often have you been asked, "How much money did the golf tournament bring in?" or "How much did the spring appeal raise?" How do you answer these questions? There are two ways.

When people have ideas about what fundraising activities they want to try in the next year, they usually base the amount of dollars that can be raised on a gross income figure. You hear something like, "ABC organization raised a hundred thousand dollars through their apple festival. Why don't we do one, too?" Gross income is total revenues raised. Board and development committee volunteers are often lured by these numbers. Fundraisers often use this number to prove their worth, like in job interviews and performance evaluations. The numbers can be impressive when you use gross income as the basis for your fundraising success. But gross income does not give the whole picture. We have met fundraisers who raise a lot of gross income, but their organizations still lose money.

To really know if you raised money, you need to consider the costs to raise the money and talk about net income. Net income is total revenues minus expenses. Net income shows a more accurate picture of the dollars raised. Joanne once interacted with an organization that raised $1 million every year through its gala. Woohoo, right? No. It actually cost it $1.25 million to put on the affair. That means it lost $250,000 on the event. Every year! No wonder the organization was in financial trouble.

And we can give example after example of this occurrence. If you want to start delving into why your fundraising program raises so much money but your organization still has financial problems, look at your costs to raise the money. Look at your net income. We talk in more detail about costs in **Chapter Four**.

When you look at the dollars raised, you want to look at how your fundraising program performed overall within a year and how much each fundraising channel brought in. That way, you can compare the financial performance of activities to each other and start to get a feel for what is working for you and what is not. There are other factors involved in creating a fundraising plan and schedule of activities, and you shouldn't make decisions just based on net income. For example, you also want to look at other goals the activity may meet and the benefits it yields. We cover optimizing resources in **Chapter Seven**.

Measuring Donations Garnered

To really grow your organization's fundraising income, look at how much money was raised *and* at the number of people giving. To raise more money, get your current donors to give more, get new donors to give, or attain some combination of the two. There are no other ways to influence your giving totals. So, don't only look at the amount of money raised and the amount of money raised per channel. Look at how many people are giving overall and through what activity. This will give you some idea of what fundraising activities are the most popular, a preliminary indication of your potential for attracting new donors.

Notice we said preliminary. Because getting donors to give one time is not the whole story. You want them to make that second, third, and ongoing gift too. We explore donor acquisition and donor retention in **Chapter Three**.

Data Collection, Recordkeeping, and Reporting

Instead of keeping your data in an Excel file, we recommend investing in good fundraising or donor management software. There are many useful reports you can pull with a good fundraising software program. One low-cost option Joanne has used is Eleo. For more sophisticated database management, many fundraising professionals we know invest in DonorPerfect, Bloomerang, and Blackbaud Raiser's Edge NXT, other popular sophisticated software programs. There are tons of others out there with a wide range of prices. Whatever software you choose, make sure it has all the functionality you need (a good starting point is the data collection and reporting needs mentioned in this book) and good donor tracking capabilities. You want to know how many years a donor has been giving and in what amounts. Have they increased or decreased their giving? Or did they stop giving suddenly? You need to know how you're doing in donor relations to design the interventions you need to get the best results. You want a donor software package that not only meets your needs now but will also suit you as your fundraising program grows. Get demos from several software companies and talk to other users to find the right program for you. And check into hidden costs, such as how much it will cost to convert your current data. Also, look into whether there are any specific modules you might need, such as membership, event management, or grant management, that have extra costs.

When you run your annual and year-to-date donor and donation reports, at the very least, compare this year's budgeted goals to this year's performance and this year's performance to last year's performance. You want to examine year-to-date comparisons to see how you are progressing toward your goal and make adjustments as necessary. You can go back even further, say five years, to see long-term trends. Long-term trends help you see your rate of growth over the years. Use the average rate of growth over the years to forecast your upcoming year's rate of growth. Often, the best predictor of future performance is past results.

Wrapping It Up

- Net income, not gross income, is the only indicator of true funds raised.
- Look at revenues raised by fundraising activity as well as the totals raised annually.
- Track the number of donors by channel to get a preliminary indication of where to pursue new donors.
- Invest in a good donor management software system.

Chapter Three

How Effective Are You with Your Donors?

In the last chapter, we talked about the two factors that you can influence to bring in the most money: the dollars raised and the number of people giving. In this chapter, we go into more depth about how to influence more people to give and how to influence current donors to give more. Formulating the goals you set for doing so starts with knowing where you are right now.

Average Gift Per Donor

The overall average gift per donor is calculated by dividing total revenues by the total number of donors. For this metric, use gross revenues. For example:

$1,000,000 gross revenues/2,000 donors = $500 average gift per donor overall.

The average gift per donor overall is useful in year-to-year comparisons. You want to see the average contribution per donor increasing and on an upward trajectory.

The overall average gift per donor can be broken down into average gift per donor by fundraising activity. It is calculated the same way the overall average gift per donor is. For example:

$250,000 total grant revenues/25 funders = $10,000 average grant donation,

$800,000 total individual donor revenues/1,275 donors = $627.45 per donor,

$150,000 special event revenues/750 participants = $200 average donation per event participant.

In this example, we can see that the highest gift amounts are given through grant funders, the most donations are through individual donors, and in between lies the special event participants. At this point, you know how much you raise through each channel, how many donors give through each activity, and the average gift per donor per activity. You can now take our preliminary analysis from our last chapter one step further. We can now say that we may want to try and increase the number of grant funders because they yield the highest average gift per donor. Or we may want to invest in our individual giving program because that is the most popular. Or we may wish to emphasize improving our special events, so they realize a higher average gift. However, the story does not end here. You still need to analyze costs and how well your resources are working for you. We talk about costs in detail in **Chapter Four**. We focus on measuring the efficiency of your resources in **Chapter Seven.**

Just a note on working to improve fundraising activities that aren't working for you as well as you'd like: rather than working on your overcoming your weaknesses, use a strengths-based approach and work with your strengths. It will take a lot less effort to see more positive results. And your staff will be more productive and feel more satisfied. Which means they may stay longer. The average tenure of a development professional today is about fourteen months. If you don't want that kind of revolving door, you need to make sure expectations are reasonable, and staff feels supported. And part of that formula is working with their strengths as opposed to against their weaknesses.

To drill down on the average gift per donor by category even further, you can take subgroups of the categories and see how each subgroup performs. Let's face it—time is your most precious commodity because there is only so much of it. Although we would like to do everything, our staff and we cannot, no matter how much of a superhero we all are. The time staff spends analyzing results to better plan for the future will pay off in the long run, so no using the excuse "we don't have time for all this evaluation!" To know how to raise the most dollars using the least resources, one strategy is to implement the specific fundraising activities that yield the highest gift per donor.

For example, how do foundation, corporate, and community group grants compare to one another? If you want to concentrate on grants, what type do you want to concentrate on?

Or your individual donors. What are the average gifts for the holiday appeal, Giving Tuesday campaign, and major gift efforts? Are the average gifts in each subgroup still rising? What is working for you, and what needs to go?

The same can be done by comparing special event to special event. Most special events have multiple components to them, such as tickets, sponsorships, donations, auctions, raffles, and the like. Be sure to drill down to those individual components to know what part of the special event you want to spend time on.

Most fundraising activities have a shelf life. Have you reached that point yet? You will know it is time to retire a certain activity if you see a multi-year downward trend of the number of donors and average gift per donor.

Donor Acquisition Rate

We all know that we need to recruit new donors. We need new donors to replace the ones lost through attrition and to grow our donor base. After all, a more extensive donor base should result in a larger pool of overall donations. Remember the price and volume sales analogy? Acquiring new donors is, hopefully, increasing the volume of gifts you receive.

To thoroughly analyze your acquisition efforts, you need both the actual number of new donors you acquire each year as well as your donor acquisition rate. Your donor acquisition rate tells you your rate of growth. Your goal is to maintain a constant rate of growth, maybe even improving it. Knowing your trends in donor growth can help you forecast donor base growth when you are setting goals.

You can calculate your donor acquisition rate by dividing the difference between the number of donors this year minus the number of donors last year by the number of donors last year. For example:

1,275 donors this year – 1,260 donors last year/1,260 total d0nors last year = 1.2 percent.

The current industry average donor acquisition rate is 0.8 percent. More detailed statistics by size and type of agency are collected by fundraising software agencies, combined, and then released by the Fundraising Effectiveness Project. The Fundraising Effectiveness Project is a free product of the Association of Fundraising Professionals.

Donor Retention Rate

Donor acquisition, though, does not tell the whole story. Donor retention is equally, if not more, important to calculate. Your donor retention rate tells you the percentage of your donor base that made a second or subsequent gift. An optimal donor retention rate hovers right around 80 percent, give or take a few percentage points.

It is much cheaper to retain a donor than acquire one. In fact, it typically costs six times as much to acquire a new donor as it does to retain an existing donor. Therefore, contrary to popular opinion, you will raise more money by increasing your donor retention rate instead of your donor acquisition rate. Don't get me wrong. You need donor acquisition. Life happens, and people can't donate anymore for various reasons— they die, move, lose interest, financial circumstances change, and so on. You need new donors to replace those lost through attrition. But the majority of your fundraising investment should focus on retaining donors as opposed to acquiring donors. Most nonprofits have poor donor retention rates and spend more money raising the same amount of money than they need to. If you invest in improving your donor retention rate, your costs to raise a dollar go down, increasing your net income. We talk more about costs in **Chapter Four**.

Your overall donor retention rate is calculated by dividing the total number of donors last year by the number of repeat donors this year. For example:

600 repeat donors this year/1,260 donors last year = 47.6 percent

The above example means that for every 100 donors that nonprofit acquires, 52.4 of them will *not* give again. That's more than half their total donor base. This means you are recreating more than half your donor base every year. That's a lot of time, effort, and money. Want to raise more money with fewer resources? Focus on improving your donor retention rate.

The average industry overall donor retention rate is a poor 45.5 percent. The first-time donor retention rate is even more dismal at 20.2 percent. No wonder many nonprofits are struggling! For every 100 donors they acquire, only a little more than 20 will give again.

To show how improved donor retention affects fundraising results, consider the following example, where raising $50,000 actually results in more organizational income than raising $100,000.

	Amount Raised	Average cost to Raise	Total Cost to Raise	Final Results
50 percent retained donors	$50,000	$0.20	$10,000	$40,000
50 percent new donors	$50,000	$1.20	$60,000	($10,000)
Total	$100,000	-	$70,000	*$30,000*

	Amount Raised	Average cost to Raise	Total Cost to Raise	Final Results
80 percent retained donors	$40,000	$0.20	$8,000	$32,000
20 percent new donors	$10,000	$1.20	$11,200	($1,200)
Total	**$50,000**	-	$19,200	*$30,800*

Go ahead and run your numbers. See how much more money you can raise by investing in donor retention efforts instead of a heavier emphasis on donor acquisition. For practical ideas on recruiting and engaging donors, read the ***Nonprofit Quick Guide: How to Find New Donors and Get Them to Give Again***.

Data Collection, Recordkeeping, and Recording

When you run your monthly reports, always run your average gift per donor, donor acquisition, and donor retention rates. Make sure your data entry is up to date. And make sure that you are comparing this year's year-to-date to last year's year-to-date. If you need to teach your board, executive director, or development committee volunteers what these rates tell you, then do it. Knowing these rates and basing your decision-making on them means relying on objective data instead of what you think or feel. Using objective data gives you credibility and objectively supports the decisions you make. It is less risky than following an idea that has no basis in facts.

And if you notice substantial deviation in your trends, note why. For example, a change in executive directors often leads to poorer fundraising results. Or a recession hits and affects your donors' ability to give. Or you have a fire, or a pandemic hits and operations shut down. On the positive side, maybe you changed your holiday appeal that resulted in higher average donations. You want to go back and know what circumstances or interventions caused the deviations, good or bad. You want to plan better for the next time there is an unexpected change in circumstances. You also want to know what actions to continue or discontinue to maximally positively influence fundraising results.

Wrapping It Up

◆ Look at your average gift-per-donor trends. If you have a downward trajectory, change what you are doing.

◆ Invest in specific fundraising pursuits that raise the average gift per donor.

◆ Use a strengths-based approach when designing your fundraising interventions.

◆ Know when to retire specific fundraising activities.

◆ Focus on your efforts on donor retention just as much or more than donor acquisition.

Chapter Four

How Much Cost Are You Incurring?

As we said in **Chapter One**, net income is a better indicator of monies raised than gross income. Net income takes into account the costs associated with raising funds, while gross income doesn't. You can increase net income by either increasing your revenues or decreasing your expenses. In fact, the fastest and least expensive way to increase your income is by reducing costs. This chapter talks about the cost measurements that are important to monitor so that you can make data-driven decisions about increasing or decreasing costs.

Direct and Indirect Costs

When most fundraisers think about their fundraising costs, they think about their direct costs as opposed to their total costs. Total costs are made up of direct *and* indirect costs. Direct costs are those costs directly associated with the fundraising activities themselves. Indirect costs are all the other costs associated with implementing a development program, like fundraising staff and administrative support salaries, and a portion of rent, utilities, phone, office supplies, IT, accounting, human resources, and executive management expenses. For the most accurate accounting, take into account both direct and indirect, or total, costs.

If you don't take into account total costs, you may lose money on a fundraising activity while thinking that you are making money. We see this all the time in grant writing. Nonprofit grant budgets often only list direct program costs, not mentioning any indirect costs at all. When the award comes, it only covers, then, a portion of the total organizational expenses used to implement the program. There is no money for indirect costs anywhere because they were not included in the program cost calculations. So, while it looks like getting that grant is a good thing, if you don't have a way to cover your indirect costs, you actually lose money.

To avoid situations like this in all your fundraising activities, always use total costs, not just direct costs, in your calculations. After all, your agency, no matter how small it is, incurs some sort of rent, utilities, phone, office supplies, IT, human resource, accounting, and executive management expenses. And those expenses need to be covered for your agency to grow. And agency growth means more mission will be met. And more mission being met is attractive to donors. And being attractive to donors means more money being donated. And more money being donated is what you work so hard to do. Start that upward cycle. Always calculate your total costs and base your metrics on them.

And don't forget opportunity costs. Having a staff person spend six months coordinating a special event that raises forty thousand dollars not only eats up a lot of indirect costs but incurs the cost of what might have been done instead. Think about how much you might have raised if that staff person spent that time scheduling major gift calls, seeking business donations, or working with board members to cultivate major donors.

Costs to Raise One Dollar

It takes money to make money. Fundraising involves an investment today that produces results tomorrow. Most often, you incur costs before you start realizing revenues, particularly staff costs. What results are reasonable to expect from your investment? How do you know your fundraising staff are doing their job? What does the data tell you?

Generally speaking, to raise $1 through various activities it costs:

◆ Capital campaigns and major gifts, including labor: $0.10
◆ Grant writing, including labor: $0.20
◆ Direct mail renewal, including labor (with a 50 percent or better return rate): $0.20
◆ Special events, not including labor: $0.50
◆ Direct mail acquisition, including labor (with a 1 percent or better return rate): $1.25

To calculate your costs to raise $1, divide your fundraising expenses by your fundraising revenues. For example:

$300,000 fundraising expenses/$1,000,000 fundraising revenue = $0.30 to raise $1.

You want to calculate both your overall cost as well as your costs by fundraising channel. You want to know your overall costs so you can budget correctly. You want to know how much it is costs to raise $1 via your different fundraising activities so that you know which areas you can improve on. You will use gross revenues as your revenue number. For the most accurate results, use your total costs as your expenses number. If you use total costs as your expenses number and you can get your cost to raise $1 below the industry averages, you will be doing quite well. Both your direct and indirect costs will be accounted for. Just note that the average cost to raise $1 through special events of $0.50 does not include labor. If you include your labor costs in that calculation, your cost to raise $1 may well be over $1. In our experience, once you account for salaries, most special events lose money or, at best, break even.

If your cost to raise $1 is more than these averages, you want to work on streamlining your fundraising program and see where you can cut costs. Track your trends over time to monitor progress toward your goals. Remember, changes in your fundraising program and its procedures will probably take time.

Just a note on cutting costs: do not cut *necessary* expenses. Necessary expenses include things like ongoing training and administrative support. Studies prove that fundraisers who engage in continuing professional development raise more money than those who don't. And good administrative support is crucial to maintaining tight fundraising operations. Yes, fundraising professionals can perform their own administrative tasks. But at what cost? Paying an administrative support professional to conduct the myriad of administrative tasks involved in fundraising generally costs less than paying a development professional to do the same thing. For a more detailed discussion on raising money through cost-cutting, see our ***Nonprofit Quick Guide: Seven Simple Strategies to Creating a Wildly Successful Fundraising Program.***

If you are at or below the industry averages, then you want to maintain your current program. If your costs are where you want them to be, you increase the amount of revenues you want to raise and then increase your expenses correspondingly.

Donor Costs

Other cost metrics you should be aware of are your cost to acquire a donor and the cost to retain a donor. We suggest further breaking down those costs by fundraising channel. Then compare the costs to acquire a new donor and retain a current donor across the various fundraising activities. See what your least expensive way to acquire new donors is.

In **Chapter Two**, we talked about making preliminary decisions about allocating resources to grow your donor base based on the number of donors per fundraising activity. Now you have more information. You can now also factor in the costs to recruit new donors per fundraising activity.

To calculate your cost to acquire a donor, divide the expenses used to recruit new donors by the number of new donors. For example:

$45,000 new-donor recruitment expenses/(4,200 donors this year – 4,000 donors last year) = $225 cost to recruit a new donor.

You calculate the costs of retaining a donor by dividing your normal fundraising expenses by the number of recurring donors. For example:

$120,000 recurring fundraising costs/1,880 recurring donors = $63.83 cost per recurring donor.

Of course, these costs are high because they include salaries and indirect expenses. Notice how much more expensive it is to recruit donors than retain donors, given the assumptions that this agency is spending a total of $165,000 on its fundraising program, and it had 4,000 total donors last year and 4,200 this year. You also know its donor acquisition rate is 5 percent, and its donor retention rate is 44.8 percent (remember our donor acquisition and retention rate formulas from **Chapter Three**?).

Run your own numbers and see your own results. Find out what it costs to recruit, as opposed to retaining, a donor.

Data Collection, Recordkeeping, and Reporting

To run numbers like this, make sure your recordkeeping is accurate and up to date. Take the time to enter your financial as well as donor data. Run the numbers monthly. Account for your total expenses, not just your direct ones. Find out how much it really costs to raise one dollar. Benchmark your fundraising performance to averages and see where you fall. See what fundraising channels are the least expensive for you to implement. Budget realistically, accounting for your nonprofit's current expenses. Allow time for improvement. Create realistic fundraising goals based on the ratio of revenue to costs. Make sure your team has enough resources to do what you want them to do. And then evaluate your and your team's performance using objective criteria based on the data. Support your team and stop the fourteen-month revolving door.

Wrapping It Up

- When you calculate your costs, use your total costs rather than only your direct costs.
- Benchmark your and your team's performance against industry averages. Allow a reasonable amount of time for improvement.
- When you cut costs, remember professional development and administrative expenses are often worth their investment.
- Research how much it costs your nonprofit to recruit and retain donors. Allocate resources so that you realize the most amount of money using the least amount of resources.
- Create a budget with enough resources for you and your team to reach your goals. Base your decisions on objective data.

Chapter Five

Measuring Your Marketing Endeavors

Fundraising, nonprofit marketing, and for-profit marketing are similar to each other in many ways. Fundraising is concerned with building donor relationships that result in charitable contributions. Nonprofit marketing is concerned about building community relationships that result in beneficial resources for the organization. For-profit marketing is about building customer relationships that result in sales. Both fundraising and for-profit marketing are concerned with the interactions that result in the exchange of money. Both nonprofit and for-profit marketing are interested in attracting people not currently associated with them to their cause. Fundraising, nonprofit marketing, and for-profit messages need to rise above the environmental noise to be heard. Both nonprofits and for-profits struggle to get their message noticed in all the fray. Both marketing and fundraising work to make the processes of finding donors and customers, interacting with them, and exchanging resources as easy as possible. There is a lot of overlap between fundraising, nonprofit marketing, and for-profit marketing. In many ways, borrowing concepts from the marketing world leads to better fundraising.

There are significant differences, though. The bottom line for nonprofits is mission impact, whereas the bottom line for for-profit businesses is profit. A nonprofit exists for the public good and is funded by public monies. A for-profit exists to fulfill the demand for a product or service desired by its customers and is sustained by sales. A nonprofit's income is rarely taxed. A for-profit's income is. The purposes of the nonprofit and corporate boards are also different. The ultimate authority for a nonprofit is the public, as represented by a board of community members—typically unpaid volunteers. The ultimate authority for a business is the owner, who receives the proceeds of the company. For a corporation, it is the stockholders who are the beneficiaries. Surely fundraising and nonprofit marketing are very distinctive from for-profit marketing.

All of which means that fundraising, nonprofit marketing, and for-profit marketing share some performance indicators while diverging on others. We have talked about the main metrics you need to know to make budget decisions, allocate resources toward pursuing specific activities, and evaluate the performance of your fundraising program.

We now turn your attention to key metrics we can borrow from marketing to drastically improve your fundraising results.

Key Performance Indicators

Key Performance Indicators, also known as KPIs, are tracked numerical marketing metrics used to measure progress toward your goal within specific marketing channels. The marketing channels we will discuss include your website, email campaigns, and social media efforts.

Website Metrics

Go into Google Analytics or other tracking software and track the number of website visitors you get per month. And you want to know the number of unique, as opposed to returning, visitors you have, too. If you are using paid means to drive traffic to your site, you will also want to know how many organic visitors (people who find you through unpaid means) and how many paid visitors you had. In addition, you want to monitor which pages had the most hits and how long people stayed on those pages. What you are looking for are clues to what is appealing about frequently visited and read pages. Your ideal is to have increased traffic to your site over time, with more people visiting and reading key pages. For fundraising purposes, this means your donation pages. However, the look, feel, and friendliness of your overall site impacts single-page performance. So, make sure that you design your donation pages in conjunction with a marketing professional. If you don't have a marketing professional on staff, we suggest you invest in a good website design firm to help you. Design accounts for 90 percent of the trust people place in the companies they are researching through websites. It is worth the investment for your site to generate the most trust possible.

You will also want to know how many of your website visitors end up donating to your cause. Track your results over time. Your goal is to increase traffic to your site and, to the point, your donation page. You also want to measurably increase the rate of conversion of visitors to donors.

Offering downloadable tools is often an excellent way to engage donors. For example, "10 ways you can help community recycling efforts." Track how many people are downloading them and calculate your conversions, that is, how many times the offer results in donations, volunteer engagement, or referrals.

Email Metrics

For email campaigns, you want to keep track of the number of emails sent, open rate, click-through rate, bounce rate, and response rate. If you're using something like Constant Contact, Mailchimp, or ActiveCampaign, your email provider will track and can provide these statistics. If you have a large email list, you can do some A/B testing of your emails to see which version of your email performs better. If you don't have a large list, then experiment with subject headings, layout, pictures of graphics, content, and time of day sent. But only change one variable at a time for long enough to get reliable results. Then experiment with another variable. With this experimentation, when the time comes to send out your fundraising campaign, you will know what works best for your organization.

Make sure that you clean your email address list often. You want as few bad email addresses as possible, so you get an accurate picture of just how effective your campaigns are. Plus, high bounce rates can lead to your communications being categorized as spam. You don't want to risk your fundraising email campaign being labeled as spam. So, make sure you scrub your list often.

After your campaign, make sure you track the number of donations and the number of donors who gave during the campaign. Also, have your revenue and expenses actuals. You will want to calculate the average gift per donor, average cost per donor, and cost to raise one dollar. Compare this year's numbers to last year's numbers. You will want to know trends as well as your email donor acquisition costs. Use this information to evaluate the effectiveness of using email in terms of popularity and costs versus other channels.

If you want to build on the efficacy of your email campaign, you can follow up your email communications with other email communications or more personal phone contact. We recommend that you send at least three email communications or send an email, follow up with a phone message, and then send another email, only contacting donors that haven't yet responded to the previous communications. Of course, when donors do respond positively, make sure you thank them immediately. Thanking your donors within forty-eight hours of the donation while the memory of making the donation is still fresh in their minds is the number one way to help get a second donation.

Social Media Metrics

Social media is a good tool for getting your message out to a large number of people. The key to reaching a lot of people is in gathering followers to your page. And likes and shares of your posts. When you post on social media, you will want to track your number of followers, likes, shares, and responses. For best results, like, share, and respond to those who have posted responses to you. Engage people in conversation.

Use lots of pictures when you post. Pictures generate interest. Personal posts generate more interest than fact-based ones. Short posts are better than long ones. Generate interest in the community impact your agency is making; that is, how your organization is improving the human condition, one person at a time. Social media is a great way to make your nonprofit human and relatable.

If you do a fundraising campaign on social media, make sure to track your results. The jury is still out on how effective a fundraising tool social media is. What everyone agrees on, though, is that social media can highlight your impact in the community and engage people in your cause, augmenting your fundraising efforts.

Data Collection, Recordkeeping, and Reporting

Most of your tracking and reporting will come from Google Analytics or other tracking software, your email provider, and your social media platform. You want to associate your marketing activities with your fundraising performance to see if and how strong the relationship is between the two. Marketing generally enhances fundraising. Leverage your resources, reduce organizational costs, and magnify outcomes by intertwining your fundraising efforts with your agency's marketing campaigns. Work in conjunction with marketing and coordinate your efforts.

Wrapping It Up

- Although fundraising, nonprofit marketing, and for-profit marketing share many concepts, you must also consider their many differences.
- Website, email, and social media key performance indicators are useful to analyze a fundraising campaign's impact.
- The design of your website accounts for 90 percent of the trust developed by visitors to the website. Develop your donation page with the input of a website design professional.

◆ To learn the most successful email configuration, experiment with subject headings, layout, pictures, graphics, content, and time of day sent, changing only one variable at a time.

◆ Scrub your mailing lists often.

◆ Social media augments fundraising efforts and enhances financial results.

Chapter Six

Evaluating the Efficacy of Your Processes

I n **Chapter Five**, we talked about how fundraising and marketing are similar to and different from one another. In this chapter, we continue to borrow from the field of marketing, but with a twist. We borrow the concepts of the customer journey and customer experience, revising them to reflect the donor focus of fundraising.

The Donor Journey and Conversion Metrics

The customer journey is the overall series of interactions a person takes from first becoming aware of a company to the point of purchase. It lays out all the steps a person takes to result in a sale, along with the processes and procedures involved in completing each individual step. To measure the efficiency of the processes and procedures, typical marketing KPIs (remember **Chapter Five**?) include metrics about the number of conversions at each step of the process. In other words, the percentage of people completing each step that move on to engage in the next interaction. In this way, businesses can see where people tend to drop off in the series of interactions and develop solutions designed to keep potential customers in the pipeline. The purpose of customer-journey mapping and calculating the related conversion rates is to better manage the customer pipeline and increase sales.

The donor journey is the series of interactions a person takes from first becoming aware of your nonprofit to the point of donating. The series of steps that result in a donation will be different from nonprofit to nonprofit. Because most nonprofits have many ways for donors to interact with them, mapping and managing the donor journey can be quite complicated.

The first thing to do in mapping your donor journey is to write down all the points of entry. For example, potential donors can be volunteers, employees, board members, advocates, community collaborators, business professionals, neighbors, friends, relatives, or people we serve, among others. How do these people find you? How do you reach out to them? How easy is it to respond to you? Do you have a call to action, that is, a message inviting them to interact with you? What is that process? How easy is it to interact with you? Can you or the appropriate person be easily reached? How? Through what channels? Do you have a backup plan if one channel becomes blocked—say your website crashes or your phones go down?

Then you go to the second step and do the same thing. How can people continue to interact with you? What do you ask of them? What can they expect of you? Do you explain their commitment? Do you explain your commitment? Do you offer a way for them to provide feedback? How onerous is your process? What are the barriers to experiencing a satisfactory interaction? How do you know? Have you checked? Do you start another call to action to proceed to the next step? How user-friendly is that process?

And then the third step, the fourth, and so on, noting the processes and procedures in place at each step and evaluating their efficacy and efficiency. And when you have it all mapped out, test the process to make sure actual results are what you expected and that the process is consistent across a variety of users and user conditions.

Then track the number of potential donors who go through each step and calculate your conversion rates. This is most easily done through CRM (constituent relationship management) software, such as HubSpot or Salesforce. Some donor management software systems have CRM components to them as well. Just make sure that the marketing software you buy serves the unique needs of nonprofits, and any donor management software you are contemplating for CRM has robust marketing features. There are many CRM products on the market at a variety of price points. Investing in a good CRM system will make performing the marketing activities you need to be the most successful at fundraising easier. A good CRM system also makes it easier to monitor, track, and manage complex donor journeys.

The Donor Experience and Measuring Satisfaction

The donor experience results from the series of interactions mapped out in the donor journey, your brand touchpoints, and your physical environment. The outcomes can be measured on five different planes: rational, emotional, sensory, physical, and spiritual. A positive donor experience happens when interactions meet expectations.

To establish clear expectations, all of your organizational materials, not only the promotional ones, need to communicate a consistent message. Your agency's message needs to be consistent across all internal and external communications, over time, and across the rational, emotional, sensory, physical, and spiritual planes. Communicate the same message, from your logo to your training manuals to your marketing vehicles. For a detailed discussion on communicating a consistent message to the community, see our *Nonprofit Quick Guide: The Surprisingly Easy Steps to Receiving Robust Community Support*.

You want the donor experience to be as satisfying as possible so that the donor will continue interacting with you and give again. This means that you need ways to engage donors after they make their donations. At the very least, thank them. And when you thank them, thank them immediately. And then have a call to action, that is, ask them to do something else. And when they do the next thing, report on the results of their actions. Let them know the impact they made-for the people you serve, not your organization. Remember, always focus on mission as opposed to money. You want to keep the donor journey going, hopefully resulting in another, or bigger, donation. Keep the cycle going of thanking, making a call to action, reporting results, and thanking again. For ways to engage your donors and keep them giving, read our *Nonprofit Quick Guide: How to Find New Donors and Get Them to Give Again*.

Of course—and it happens all the time—what you think may not be what your donors think. Ever heard the phrase, "I know that you think you know what I said, but I'm not sure that what you heard is what I meant?" Well, as we said, it happens all the time. To really know what your donors think, you need to ask them about their perceptions. Ask them if they find interactions with you satisfactory or rewarding. Ask them how you can improve the process. Ask them if you are providing them with something they need or want and find meaningful. Ask them how they feel at each stage in interaction. Ask them about what they like and don't like about the look and feel of your materials. Ask them what they think your words and concepts mean. Ask them how comfortable they are with the language you use. Ask them for their input at every touchpoint. And then ask them if you understand them correctly. Check your interpretation of what they said. Your goal is to design and revise a series of interactions that you know for sure donors and potential donors will understand and enjoy participating in. And the only way to know what satisfies them is to ask them.

That doesn't mean you constantly ask questions. It means you ask until you get a representative sample of your donors and potential donors. It may mean you send out a questionnaire. Or maybe you conduct several focus groups. You may facilitate one-on-one interviews. Possibly you administer a social media poll. There are many ways to ask for feedback. Just make sure you get the feedback before you go to all the time, trouble, and expense of designing or redesigning a system that you don't know will be pleasing to your potential donor base. The only way to know for sure is to ask.

Data Collection, Recordkeeping, and Recording

Tracking the customer journey and brand touchpoints can be overwhelming. So can recording numerous responses to questionnaires and surveys. You will need pretty sophisticated software to efficiently keep track of all that data and run reports. A good CRM system will help immensely, whether you use marketing software that caters to nonprofits or donor management software with robust CRM features. A good CRM system will also have other features, like automated email sequences, which save time when conducting large email campaigns and integrating fundraising with other agency communications.

In addition to the KPIs discussed in the last chapter, add conversion rates and satisfaction measures to your cadre of evaluation metrics. Use your metrics to really figure out where you can implement interventions that will increase the return on your resources and/or use the least resources possible. Your ever-present goal is to achieve the most amount of impact with the least drain on resources. You want to grow your donor base and increase donations to expand your agency's capacity to meet more mission. You want the "more mission—more money—more mission—more money" cycle to take hold. Map your donor journey. Look at your overall messaging. Create expectations that are realized. Be sure that your potential donors will be satisfied. Use the data and tools available to you to knock your fundraising results out of the park.

Wrapping It Up

◆ Mapping the donor journey and tracking conversion rates helps you design a user-friendly fundraising system that produces results.

◆ Test your processes and procedures to ensure the actual results are the expected results. Conduct multiple tests to ensure consistency across different users and their conditions.

◆ Make sure *all* agency messages are consistent. Go beyond your marketing materials.

◆ Engage your donors by thanking them and presenting another call to action again and again.

◆ Check your assumptions and confirm your perceptions by asking your donors.

◆ Investing in a good CRM platform will help you use fewer resources to raise more money.

Chapter Seven

Optimizing Your Resources

In **Chapter Two** we talked about the difference between gross and net income and how net income is a better indicator of fundraising success than gross income. We also began our discussion about influencing the relationship between the amount of donations and the number of donors. In **Chapter Three** we covered how calculating and tracking your average gift per donor and donor acquisition rates can help guide your resource allocation decisions. We also told you about the drastic effect small improvements in your donor retention rate can have. In **Chapter Four**, we started factoring costs into our decision-making, talking about direct and indirect costs, costs to raise a dollar, and the costs to acquire and retain donors. **Chapters Five and Six** led us to discussions about marketing concepts and metrics and how, when employed, they enhance fundraising efforts. We covered common website, email, social media, and conversion KPIs. We also spent time focusing on the importance of testing our processes, soliciting donor feedback, and confirming our perceptions. In this chapter, we explore return on investment and profit margin, our final two essential gauges.

Return on Investment

Return on investment tells you how well your resources are financially performing. To calculate return on investment, you divide net income by expenses. The ratio expresses what percentage of your gross revenues are devoted to costs. For example:

$1,000,000 net income for that activity/$20,000 in expenses for that activity = 500 percent return on investment.

In other words, for every dollar you spend, you earn five. You might find a return on investment like this in your grant writing or individual giving program.

Return on investment is an excellent financial metric to use when making final decisions on allocating resources to individual fundraising activities and determining your fundraising mix.

You look at net income first. Which activity yields the most income? Then you look at the return on investment to see which activities are giving you the most bang for the buck. If the activities that result in the highest net income are the same activities that give you the highest return on investment, congratulations! You are using the fewest amount of resources to raise the most money. If not, you may want to consider changing your fundraising strategy.

As you may have noticed, your return on investment is related to the cost to raise a dollar, which we discussed in **Chapter Four**. Before changing your fundraising mix based on return on investment, make sure your cost to raise a dollar through your different fundraising activities is near the industry average. You want to make sure that you are not changing your mix to do more of what needs fixing. In other words, you want to eliminate any of the activity's operational inefficiencies before you allocate resources to do more of it.

Return on investment is a readily understood metric by many business professionals. When you approach business executives to support your organization and its work, highlight the return on investment metric. Return on investment terminology may also be the preferred terminology when talking to your board about fundraising performance, since many board members are business professionals.

Profit Margin

Profit margin is calculated by dividing net income by revenues. Profit margin tells you what percentage of gross revenues are not devoted to costs. In other words, what percentage of gross revenues is profit? For example:

$100,000 net income for that activity/$120,000 in revenues for that activity = 83 percent profit margin.

In other words, for every $1 you raised, $0.83 was profit. That's a pretty good margin. Imagine how much money you would raise if all your fundraising efforts yielded that sort of profit!

No, profit is not a dirty word in the nonprofit arena. Nonprofits *can* make profits (though we usually call them "net revenue"). They just have to invest the profits back into the mission for the inurement of the public, as opposed to for-profit companies, where profits go to the owners or stockholders. To have resources to pour back into your mission, you must make a profit. Where else is the money going to come from? It's okay to be growing and doing well. Making profits is how you get there. In fact, donors are more likely to support a healthy, growing organization than they are to throw money into a "sinking ship." So, get rid of that "tin cup" mentality.

Profit margin is highly related to return on investment. And, like return on investment, it is good for making comparisons and resource allocation decisions.

And, just like return on investment, the profit margin is highly related to the cost to raise a dollar. As with the cost of raising a dollar, the profit margin is a good, objective, data-driven tool for setting attainable revenue expectations.

Data Collection, Recordkeeping, and Reporting

Since the return on investment and profit margin are financial metrics, you will collect data from your nonprofit's financial records, mainly budgets. It is imperative that your fundraising team is talking to your financial team. They need to coordinate the formulation of the development budget and verify financial performance with each other. It is also imperative that your development team check their data with the finance team. You want to make sure that not only are your budgets the same but your recordkeeping lines up, too. You do not want to get to a board meeting and have a financial report and fundraising report with different numbers. That will only confuse board members, especially those who are less financially savvy. And when conflicting information is coming from other parts of the agency, you don't look like you have control over what is going on. Your leadership may be questioned. Not something you want to happen! So, take the time to get your finance and fundraising reports to tell the same story using the same numbers.

We have often found conflict in nonprofits between development officers and financial officers, who seem to be speaking different languages. To prevent this conflict, make friends with your finance officer, and learn more about their role. Talk about expectations on both sides. Learn about accounting and teach them about fundraising. Listen to their challenges and explain yours. Build a relationship based on understanding and mutual respect.

Wrapping It Up

◆ Return on investment tells you how efficiently you are using resources.

◆ Calculating the return on investment of your different fundraising activities can help you make resource allocation decisions.

◆ The return on investment metric is widely understood within the business community. Highlight your returns on investment when interacting with business professionals.

◆ Nonprofits *can* make profits, which are then used to invest in mission, grow organizational capacity, and meet more mission.

◆ Make sure the numerical data from fundraising and financial reports tell the same story.

Chapter Eight

Bringing It All Together

Although it may not be the most exciting part of fundraising, knowing how to use essential metrics can significantly increase your level of fundraising success. Collecting pertinent data and analyzing the associated fundraising, marketing, and financial metrics can help you budget realistically, make resource allocation decisions, set and meet fundraising goals, benchmark your or someone else's performance, evaluate your results, and help you formulate solutions when outcomes are less than optimal. In addition, the objectivity inherent in numerical measurements supports data-based decision-making, taking much guesswork out of the equation. Plus, data-based decision-making gives you credibility, enhancing your position as a leader in your agency. That's a lot that numbers can do. Understand and utilize your essential metrics.

When you create your fundraising budget, you want to make sure you allocate enough resources for you and your team to reach your goals. Knowing how much revenues your specific fundraising activities generate and how much it costs you to implement those activities, you can project revenues based on your expense budget. Expense projections are usually easier to develop than revenue projections. When you calculate your expenses, use your total costs as opposed to only your direct costs. You don't want to spend more money than you're bringing in. Make sure those indirect costs are accounted for.

When you budget, invest in the specific fundraising pursuits that raise the average gift per donor. Also, make sure to set aside resources and budget for donor retention and acquisition efforts. Donors don't just magically appear and stay. They need ongoing cultivation to get engaged and give again. To help make decisions, calculate the return on investment of each of your fundraising activities. Allocate resources so that you realize the most amount of money using the least amount of resources. Robust donor management and CRM software systems produce a high return on investment, helping you use fewer resources to raise more money. So, too, with continuing education and administrative support. Investments in professional development and administrative support have been shown to improve fundraising results.

Use metrics to benchmark your and your team's performance against industry averages. If you don't measure up, allow a reasonable amount of time for improvement. It takes time to incorporate change into existing processes and procedures.

Set attainable goals and reasonable expectations. Stop the fourteen-month revolving door. Constantly bringing on new staff is quite expensive for your organization. Data-driven decisions can help you formulate reasonable and attainable financial and fundraising goals that help your staff feel productive rather than frustrated. Focus your energies on donor retention just as much or more than donor acquisition. Donor retention is less expensive than donor acquisition, yielding a greater financial return. Engage your donors by thanking them and proposing calls to action again and again.

Employing marketing concepts can enhance fundraising efforts, drastically improving fundraising results. Plan your fundraising activities to coordinate with and leverage organizational finance, marketing, and communication efforts. Make sure *all* agency messages are consistent with one another—internal, external, written, and verbal. Look at your website, email, and social media key performance indicators to analyze a fundraising campaign's impact. To discover the most effective email system, experiment with subject headings, layout, pictures, graphics, content, and time of day sent, changing only one variable at a time.

When someone tells you how much they raised, ask if it was net or gross income. Net income is a better measure of fundraising success than gross income. Look at revenues raised by each fundraising activity as well the total raised. Track the number of donors by fundraising channel to get a preliminary indication of where to pursue new donors. Also, calculate your average gift per donor per fundraising channel and track trends.

Measure your outcomes against your budget, goals, industry averages, and agency history. To avoid confusion, make sure the numerical data in your fundraising and financial reports tell the same story. Make changes if your metrics are unsatisfactory, set attainable goals and reasonable expectations, and always remember it takes time to realize significant change. Use a strengths-based approach when you implement your fundraising interventions. It will save you and your staff time and aggravation. And know when to retire specific fundraising activities. All fundraising activities have a shelf life.

Mapping the donor journey and tracking conversion rates helps you design a user-friendly fundraising system that produces favorable results. Make the donor journey as enjoyable as possible. Check your assumptions and confirm your perceptions by asking your donors about their experiences. And make sure your processes and procedures work the way you want them to. Test them to ensure that the actual results are the expected results. Conduct multiple tests to ensure consistency across different users and their conditions.

Incorporate data collection into the design of your fundraising activities. Keep up with your data entry and recordkeeping. Run and analyze the numbers regularly. Utilize metrics on an ongoing basis. Make them an integral part of your fundraising program. You will be thankful you did.

www.ingramcontent.com/pod-product-compliance
Lightning Source LLC
Chambersburg PA
CBHW071523210326
41597CB00018B/2862